IMAGES
of America

CAMDEN
AND
ROCKPORT

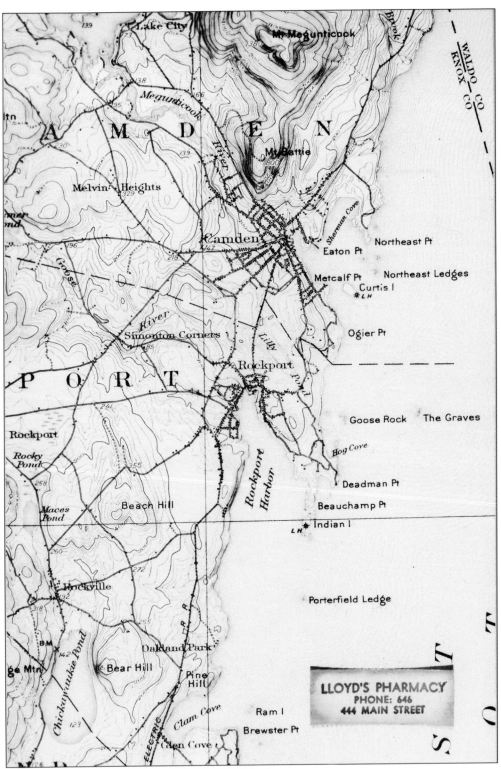

A map of Camden and Rockport.

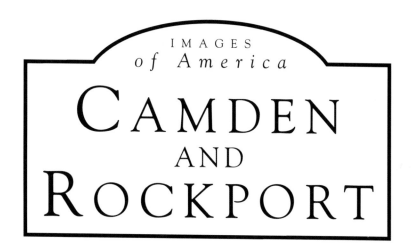

IMAGES
of America

CAMDEN
AND
ROCKPORT

Barbara F. Dyer

ARCADIA

ISBN 0-7524-0232-3

Published by Arcadia Publishing,
an imprint of the Chalford Publishing Corporation
One Washington Center, Dover, New Hampshire 03820
Printed in Great Britain

Library of Congress Cataloging-in-Publication Data applied for

OTHER PUBLICATIONS BY BARBARA F. DYER
Grog Ho! A History of Wooden Vessel Building in Camden, ME
Vintage Views of Camden, ME
History of First Congregational Church, Camden, ME

Contents

Advertisements from 1893.

6

Introduction

Picturesque Camden, Maine, so cozily snuggled at the foot of Mt. Battie and Mt. Megunticook, has been talked and written about for well over two hundred years. There are only two places from the Gulf of Mexico to the Bay of Fundy where the mountains meet the sea: Camden and Mt. Desert. Both are located in Maine.

Camden was named for Lord Camden (Charles Pratt) who had been Lord Chief Justice and Lord High Chancellor. These were two of the highest positions in Britain. He opposed his government's policy in the Revolutionary War, which made him very popular in America. He was so popular, in fact, that there are seventeen places in the United States named Camden. Perhaps you have noticed Lord Camden's coat of arms on the town side of the Camden Public Library. Just one hint . . . high people are in high places!

James Richards, the first settler of Camden, sailed into our harbor on May 8, 1769, with his wife Betsy and their African cook. James built the first log cabin between what is now Free Street and LaVerdierre's parking lot. He had come here before, with his brothers Joseph and Dodipher, to cut timber, and they loved the natural beauty of the place. He later built a frame house and applied for a permit from the "Twenty Associates" for lot #28, as shown on Fale's survey map dated 1768. He did not actually receive the lot until 1803. His parcel of land contained mill privileges on the Megunticook River and it remained in his family for many years. When James arrived, there were a few wigwams on Eaton's Point (now Wayfarer's property) and more Native Americans on Beauchamp Point.

Robert Thorndike was the next to arrive, and he settled at Goose River. When Camden was incorporated as a town in 1791, it also included Goose River (now Rockport), Clam Cove (now Glen Cove), West Camden (now West Rockport), and Rockville. Camden's interests, even then, were attracting tourists and building sidewalks. Rockport wanted to build a bridge and attract industries. Town meetings between the two factions—the "Harbor" faction (Camden) and the "Goose River" faction (Rockport)—were very lively. Most Camden residents wanted a separation, whereas Rockport residents did not. In 1891, the fight was sent to the Maine House of Representatives, in Augusta. The state senate passed an act splitting Camden into two towns. One legislator remarked "You should be celebrating a centennial instead of suing for a divorce."

Camden and Rockport are wonderful places to live in or visit.

Barbara F. Dyer

This book is dedicated in loving memory of my mother, Elizabeth Ayoube Dyer (1894–1958)

One
Evolution of Travel

Main Street in Camden had very little traffic on the day this picture was taken in 1912. People walked or drove a horse and buggy.

At a time when only a few streets had been developed, there were still many beautiful country roads. These ladies are probably strolling to a friend's for tea, taking the opportunity to chat and enjoy the beauty of nature along the way. This was a time when walking was both a necessity and good exercise as well.

A pleasant view of Rockport, at the intersection of Union Street and Russell Avenue. Notice the Carleton Hotel to the left. The Rockport Opera House is just out of view on the right.

Crossing the old bridge in Rockport to Pascal Avenue by horse and buggy, c. 1906. Goose River flows beneath the bridge. A school appears on the hill in the background. The building to the left of the bridge was later moved to Millville in Camden. The bridge had to be rebuilt after a truck crashed into it, and it looks quite different today.

"Ol' Dobbin" is shown in this picture hauling a sleigh with its owners from Main Street up Harbor Hill. In those days winter was really winter in Maine. People took good care of their horses because they were depended upon for transportation. The sleigh glided smoothly over the snowy roads.

Trolley cars were a convenient mode of transportation. In this photograph, it appears as if a horse is looking out of the window of the trolley, but he must have been standing beside the trolley as the photographer took the picture.

"Horseless carriages" and a trolley are shown among pedestrians in front of the Camden Opera House. Trolleys were the principal mode of transportation in Knox County from 1892 to 1931, with the fare being only 5¢ from town to town.

This is a view from Harbor Hill, looking at Main Street, showing people walking or traveling by horse and wagon. When Harbor Park was built, the buildings on the left were razed.

This trolley failed to negotiate a curve by the Opera House in Rockport. The motorman was killed in this incident on January 15, 1920. The author's parents were on this trolley, traveling from Camden, but fortunately they were not hurt. Only two fatal accidents happened in the trolley's thirty-nine years of operation.

The trolley barns and power house were located in Glen Cove, then a part of Rockport. It is still known as "Powerhouse Hill." Today, a picnic area encompasses some of the lower land, while berry growers and fishermen sell their products on the hill to passing motorists.

Camden, Maine. Elm Street looking South.

Then came the first automobiles to Camden. This photograph shows one chugging along in 1917, heading south beneath the canopy of elm trees that lined Elm Street. The spacious old homes remain, but the road is now Route 1 and somewhat spoiled by commercialization.

People loved the steamers that ran from Boston to Bangor, stopping at points along the way. It was exciting to meet the "Boston Boat" when it docked with its passengers and freight. In the late 1800s, the steamship company provided a ball which lit up when a boat was docking, so the light could be seen from many points in Camden. People would then hurry to the steamboat wharf and that was the excitement for the day. The line continued until 1937.

The first steamboat came into Penobscot Bay in 1823. People were worried that it would frighten all the fish, but the boat came anyway, and the fish stayed. The Eastern Steamship Wharf (pictured here, with the steamer *Camden*) was completely destroyed by fire in 1924, and a new one rebuilt the same year. After the steamboat era, the wharf was used as a mold loft during World War II. Later, it was sold as a lobster-packing plant. By May 1959 it had become a menace to navigation and was burned by the town.

Two

Resorts

Joseph Sterns, the inventor of the duplex system of telegraphy, built "Norumbega" in 1886. The "castle" was privately owned until a few years ago when it became a very unique and popular inn. Located less than a mile out of Camden, going north on Route 1, it is the most photographed place in the area.

Today, the Rockport Public Library is located on the site of the former Carleton House. The Carletons owned stores, a shipbuilding company, and a lime company in Rockport, as well as the hotel. Banquets and large parties took place in hotels such as these.

Until consumed by fire in 1903, the Ocean House had been a very large and popular resort in Camden. The town built the Camden Public Library on the site. The Ocean House well and some of the burned timbers from the hotel remain buried beneath the library grounds.

Francis Cobb II owned the spacious old Bay Point Hotel that opened on July 4, 1889. It was sold thirteen years later to the Ricker family of Poland Springs fame. They embellished the building and named it Samoset for the Pemaquid Indian who greeted (in English) the Pilgrims from the *Mayflower*. Samoset closed its doors in 1969 and a fire destroyed it in October 1972. Today, a wonderful new Samoset, built nearby, serves as a first-class hotel to the delight of many.

Hotel Edwards was built on Bayview Street in 1882. Its owners, size, and name have changed many times since then. Presently called the Camden Harbor Inn, it is located just beyond the Camden Yacht Club, and commands a spectacular view of the mountains and harbor.

Local newspapers first mentioned the Bay View House in 1801, when the Amity Lodge of Masons held its first meeting in the Benjamin Palmer Hall. About eight years later the newspapers were calling it the principal hotel in Camden. Tourists visiting the town often stayed at this wonderful place, which could seat 250 people for a banquet. On November 16, 1917, the hotel was destroyed by fire. Today, the Village Green is located here.

The Mount Battie House, first known as the Summit House, was owned by the Mt. Battie Association. Located on the summit, it became an exclusive hotel in 1900 and remained open until 1920, when it was torn down because it was no longer financially viable. The lavish parties on the top of the mountain soon became only memories.

About half a mile from Camden, headed north, is the Whitehall Inn—a first-class summer hotel. It looks the same as it did in 1912, when Edna St. Vincent Millay recited her poem *Renascence*. The summer visitors, on whom "Vincent" made such an impression, paid her way through Vassar College. She won the Pulitzer prize for poetry in 1922 and became Camden's poet laureate.

LAKE CITY INN.

CAMDEN, ME.

Guests are hereby notified that the Proprietor will not be responsible for Valuables, Money, Jewelry, Etc., unless the same are deposited in the Safe at the Office.

F. A. D. SINGHI, Manager.
GEO. B. FOUNTAIN, Landlord.

AMERICAN HOTEL GUIDE, GIVING POPULATION OF TOWNS, NAMES OF HOTELS, RATES PER DAY, IN FRONT OF THIS BOOK.

Name.	Residence.	Time.	Room.	Horse.
Continued				
Thursday Aug 10/93				
Dr D Colson	Belfast		1	✓
Friday Aug 11th 93				
Miss Kate A. Hook	Brooklyn N.Y.			✓
Mrs. C. F. Wood	Rockland			✓
Mrs A. J. Show	" "			✓
Miss E. C. Litchfield	" "			✓
Mrs H. M. Porter	Gardiner			✓
Saturday. Aug. 12d '93 B				
John Macmahon	Boston	"		✓
Sunday, Aug. 13th '93.				
Mr & Mrs H R Wood	Rockland	D		✓
Miss Wood	"	,		✓
" Acharn	Providence R.I	"		✓
Mrs Levensaler	Thomaston	"		✓
Miss Levensaler		"		✓
H F Ames	Rockland	"		✓
H C Hatch	Camden			H
J S Farnsworth	"			✓
Frank L Weeks + Lady	Rockland	·		✓

Signatures on the Lake City Inn guest register in 1893. The inn burned, after only three years of operation, in 1896.

22

Three
Harbors

On May 11, 1912, Rockport Harbor was blasted to make it deeper for the large vessels. Within a few years, "wind and water" were no longer the cheapest means of transporting goods. Times changed, as sailing vessels gave way to trains and then trucks. Large schooners no longer came into the harbor.

This photograph depicts beautiful and busy Rockport Harbor, showing vessels launching and docking, and also the lime kilns and ice sheds (where ice was stored for shipment). Amesbury Hill can be seen clearly in the background.

This picture shows what Rockport Harbor looked like ninety years ago. The lime kilns were in operation and piles of wood used for burning the lime rock are shown to the left. A two-masted vessel is docked alongside to receive the casks of lime for transportation. A part of the lime kilns business can be seen on the right.

Another lovely view of Rockport Harbor clearly shows all the buildings in the background. As with most towns in the area, trees were scarce as they had been used for fuel in homes, for burning in the kilns, for lumber to build homes, and for many other purposes over the years.

In the early years, the Rockport waterfront was not cleaned up and landscaped for beauty. Residents made their living on the harbor, and waterfront property did not have the prime value it does today.

The building to the right of this picture has a sign reading "Rockport Ice House, coal, wood, and lumber," but to read it you must have good eyes. According to the 1888 Maine Register, the company also sold hay, boots, shoes, clothing, hardware, and ships' chandlery.

It's wintertime in Rockport, Maine, 1908. All four seasons of the year are beautiful, although there are a few who claim we have two seasons—July and winter!

This photograph of Rockport Harbor shows the schooners, the business blocks, a schoolhouse, and a church. In the center of the picture is the first building constructed in the village. One man built it from granite blocks cut from one piece of rock nearby. Today, that building houses the Corner Shop.

Camden Harbor had not yet been beautified with its lovely parks at the time of this picture. The Mt. Battie House can be seen on the summit of the mountain and the anchor factory is located on the left.

Much like Rockport, Camden had a working waterfront, so its beautification was not a priority. It continued this way until c. 1930, when both towns were blessed with a generous benefactor. She provided work during the Depression and beautified both towns at the same time.

Shown here, in 1912, are lower Sea Street and the shipyard on the east side of the harbor. In the background on the left, you may notice a five-masted vessel built and ready to be launched from the Holly M. Bean Yard. Curtis Island (at that time known as Negro Island) is in the center, and Dillingham's Point is on the right.

Looking towards the shipyard on the right, we can see a steamboat being docked near a three-masted schooner. A two-masted schooner has already been hauled on the ways, as has another large boat on the other railway. This photograph was taken c. 1922.

Seen here, *c.* 1917, is a beautiful, panoramic view of the mountains meeting the sea. On the left are wharves belonging to coal and lumber yards. On the summit of Mt. Battie is a hotel, with Mt. Megunticook a little to the rear. A three-masted schooner is on the railway at the shipyard.

Steamboats, along with a two-masted and three-masted vessel, docked at the shipyard. The inner harbor did not appear to be busy on this day in 1911.

To the right is the first Eastern Steamship Wharf and in the center is Sherman's Point (this photograph was taken before any houses were built there).

This photograph of Camden Harbor in 1922 shows the steamer that made daily trips from Islesboro to Camden and back. It was before the days of the ferry service from Lincolnville Beach to Islesboro.

The view from the head of the harbor to the east side was not particularly attractive in the early days, especially at mean low tide.

The west side of Camden Harbor, seen here *c.* 1920, had buildings in the background belonging to dealers in coal, ice, hay, and lumber. In the foreground is Vanderbilt's yacht, *Tarantalia*. A private yacht of that length is seldom seen in the area today.

Looking through the birch trees from Dillingham's Point to the outer harbor. The Eastern Steamship Wharf and the mountains appear in the background. Both large and small sail boats were moored in Camden's outer harbor.

Low tide gives a clear view of the pilings that held up the wharf at the waterfront. Small boats were anchored in the calm water on the day this photograph was taken.

Before Harbor Park was developed and designed by noted landscape architect Frederick Law Olmstead, the head of the harbor appeared as it does in this picture. To the left is the Borland building, which is now on the National Register of Historic Places and known as the American Boathouse.

This photograph was taken in the first part of the twentieth century, looking across the inner harbor towards the shipyard, Negro Island, and Dillingham Point.

The Eastern Steamship Wharf can be seen very clearly in this picture. In the early 1920s there was also a pier on the western side of the harbor. Some of the large estates, known as "cottages," are shown beneath the two mountains.

The tower on Mt. Battie had been built by the time this picture was taken. Many of the buildings shown here no longer exist, and we can see that the inner harbor of Camden was much quieter than it is today.

The pier, depicted here in the foreground c. 1930s, belonged to a privately-owned estate and is no longer in existence.

Pictured here is the very rough shore line on the west side, approached from Bay View Street. The large building on the right was a joiner shed belonging to the shipyard. It has since burned, as have some of the other buildings pictured here.

Shown here are some of the houses at the lower end of Sea Street, leading to the shipyard. The darker buildings near the water are coal sheds. They were torn down about thirty years ago.

This picture shows a view of the shipyard from the waterfalls located at the back of Main Street, Camden.

A very clear picture, taken c. 1920, of the houses on Sea Street and the railways at the shipyard and steamboat wharf. In early 1900, the shipyard had only had a few buildings. Sherman's Point can be seen in the background.

An aerial photograph taken in 1946, with the shipyard in the foreground and the steamboat wharf on the right.

Seen at the head of the harbor are some dark buildings, known as the red sheds, that stood here for many years. Only one has been restored. The bushes in the foreground hide the waterfall at the end of the Megunticook River, which empties into the harbor.

Captain Frank Swift began running windjammer cruises in 1936, and retired in 1961. He would purchase an old vessel then fix it up only as much as necessary, thereby running a profitable business. There are still many windjammer cruises running in both Camden and Rockport, but today there are stringent regulations enforced by the U.S. Coast Guard.

A clear view of the Camden Shipbuilding & Marine Railway with a vessel on the ways. The property is now Wayfarer Marine, and there have been considerable changes over the past fifteen years.

Here we can see there has been a light snowfall on Harbor Park and the mountains. When Champlain visited the Penobscot Bay, during his exploration of the area, he named the Camden hills "mountains of the Bedabedec."

Pleasure and fishing boats can be seen here anchored in the harbor, viewed from the Camden Yacht Club. The famous red sheds were then still standing at the head of the harbor.

This *c.* 1950s view from the Camden Public Library shows a quiet, working harbor.

Here, we take a closer look at the windjammers from the public landing, in 1949. By then, the red sheds were deteriorating.

The public landing was not finished when this photograph was taken in 1953, and the lumber seen here is probably for the walkways. In 1953, postage on postcards was only 2¢.

The Megunticook River is seen here where it meets the falls behind Main Street. This photograph was taken from Camden's Public Landing and the view remains the same today. The Village Shop and Smiling Cow gift shop appear here just as they do today.

This view from the back porch of the Smiling Cow gift shop shows the falls by Montgomery Dam. The Camden Public Landing is on the right.

This harbor scene, photographed from Bay Road, shows how much the buildings seen here have been improved since this picture was taken.

The rustic pilings of the shipyard in Camden are made visible by the very low tide, in this scene photographed in the fall when the leaves were in color and some of the vessels were in wet storage and covered for the winter.

Four
Curtis Island

Here we see a view of Negro Island from Dillingham's Point. When the first settler, James Richards, sailed into Megunticook harbor on May 8, 1769, his wife Betsy and their African cook were with him. History records that when the cook saw the island he said, "There, that's my island." Thus it was known as Negro Island for many years.

This scene shows the lighthouse, located on the outer harbor side of Negro Island. It has been there since 1835, when George Galt built it. It is known as the guardian of Camden Harbor.

A view from Negro Island toward Mouse Island and Sherman's Point. Negro Island has always had spectacular views from every side. It is now a public area for boaters in summer.

This view of Negro Island shows the lighthouse from the ocean side, c.1912. The first keeper was H.K.M. Bowers who was there when the light was first lit in 1836.

A view from the boat shed on Negro Island, c.1918, facing in the direction of the shipyard and the steamship wharf.

This picture was taken from the island, and shows the keeper's house, light, and bell. There were eleven lighthouse keepers here from the time the lighthouse was built to the time this picture was taken.

A close-up view of the boathouse and the ways, c. 1918. To the right is Dillingham's Point, the island's nearest point of land.

Month	Day	Ships	Barks	Brigs	Schooners	Sloops	Steamers	Total number of vessels	REMARKS
	1				10			10	wind S E thick with light Breezes
	2		1		8		1	07	wind S E thick with light Breezes
	3				1	1		02	wind S E thick with light Breezes
	4			5	16	2		23	wind S W clear with light Breezes all day
	5				11	1	1	02	wind S W clear with light Breezes & pleasant weather
	6				10	1		11	wind S W clear with light Breezes
	7				1			01	wind S W clear with fresh Breezes all day
	8				10			10	wind S W thick with light Breezes
	9				5		1	06	wind S E thick with fresh Breezes & some rain
	10				4			04	wind S W clear with light Breezes
	11				10			10	wind S W clear with light Breezes all day
	12				10	1	1	12	wind S W clear with light Breezes & pleasant weather
	13				18	2		10	wind S W clear with light Breezes
	14				05			05	wind S E thick with some rain with light Breezes
	15				64			64	wind S E thick with light Breezes all day
	16				8		7		wind S E thick with rain & fresh Breezes
	17				05	1	1	07	wind S W clear with light Breezes
	18				10			10	wind S W clear with fresh Breezes
	19				05		1	06	wind S W clear with light Breezes
	20				04			04	wind S W clear with light Breezes
	21				07			07	wind S E thick with fresh Breezes & some rain
	22								wind S E thick & rain with fresh Breezes
	23				12			12	wind S E clear with light Breezes & pleasant weather
	24				5			05	wind S W clear with light Breezes & pleasant weather
	25				16	1	1	08	wind S W clear with light Breezes
	26				5		1	06	wind S E thick with light Breezes
	27				3			03	wind S E thick & foggy, raining P.M. with light Breezes
	28				10			10	wind S W clear with light Breezes
	29				10			10	wind S W clear with light Breezes
	30				4		1	05	wind S E thick & raining all day with fresh Breezes
	31				11	1		12	wind S E clear with fresh Breezes

Here we see information from one page of a log book kept from 1860 to 1863. The Office Lighthouse Board in Washington, D.C., required that a log book be kept. The log pictured here was probably kept by Joshua Bramhall when he was light keeper. (The journal is a rare find and a treasure, given to the author by a friend.)

At low tide, the ledges are as visible today as when this picture was taken, c. 1920. It is a serene setting, but the keepers had to be very self-sufficient because the weather sometimes made it impossible to go ashore.

The townspeople voted to change the name of the island in 1934, and name it for Cyrus H.K. Curtis, a great benefactor to Camden. On March 12, 1934, the name of Negro Island was officially changed to Curtis Island. When the government gave up rights to the island, three residents—Charles Lowe, Cliff O'Rourke, and Bob Davee—flew to Philadelphia to claim it for Camden. The Board of Selectmen accepted the deed to Curtis Island on September 24, 1973.

Five
Public Buildings

The U.S. government built the Camden Post Office in 1914–15, at the cost of $85,000. A copper box was placed in the corner stone, containing: Robinson's *History*, an edition of the *Camden Herald* dated July 31, 1914, a Town Report of the same year, a roster of Post Office employees (plus photographs), and a description of Camden.

The Camden Opera House was built in 1894, after the "great fire of Camden" consumed the Megunticook building. The ground-floor windows, the doors, and the archway brickwork at the front of the building were restored, between 1993 and 1995, to how they had originally looked.

This photograph was taken in 1894. In 1994 the auditorium was restored to its original, Victorian look (after various changes through the years). Its colors are cream, salmon, gold, heliotrope, and green. A chandelier was installed, duplicating the original. Going into the beautiful auditorium is like stepping one hundred years back in time.

The kitchen of the Conway House (which now belongs to the Camden-Rockport Historical Society) is pictured here with its old cooking utensils, cradle, and spinning wheel.

The Conway House, an eighteenth-century farmhouse, was restored in 1962. It was owned by Robert Thorndike Jr., from 1807 to 1825, and then by the Conway family, who were related to Camden/Rockport's Civil War hero William Conway.

The Masonic Hall, on the third floor of the "Granite" building in Rockport, was finished by William E. Carleton, an artist and decorator. He did the Victorian decoration when he returned to Rockport after working for many years in New York. He was also responsible for the artistic work in the Camden Opera House.

The town built Camden High School in 1904 to last a lifetime. The total cost of the land and building was $20,000. The fence to the left of the picture was built there because a trotting park for horse racing was located on what is now the baseball diamond. After seventy-five years, the old school had to be torn down, but it wouldn't go without a struggle. Many bought slates from the roof and other memorabilia.

Camden High School had a great football team in 1911 and the very serious expressions of the team are captured in this photograph.

The Camden High School girls were excellent at basketball. Pictured here is the team which played in 1913–14. The captain, Ritterbush (later McGrath), holds the basketball. She remained in Camden, and her two sons, Peter and Stephen, graduated from the same high school.

Camden High School is seen here many years later. As you can see, nothing had changed since it was first built, with the exception of the trotting park, which by now was gone. Thousands of students went through those doors between 1905 and 1980.

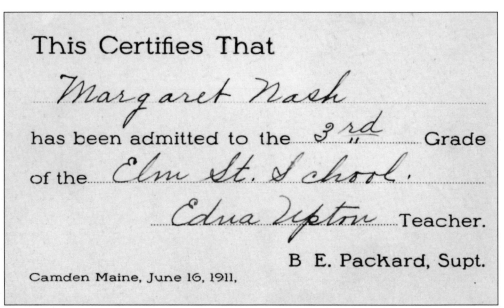

This Certifies That

Margaret Nash

has been admitted to the *3rd* Grade

of the *Elm St. School.*

Edna Upton Teacher.

B E. Packard, Supt.

Camden Maine, June 16, 1911.

At the Elm Street School, each student received a card certifying that they had passed to the next grade. Margaret Nash received one in 1911 and it was signed by her teacher, Edna Upton, and by the superintendent, B.E. Packard.

The town of Camden built the Elm Street School in 1869, and the lower grades are still using it. In this early picture the main entrance is located on School Street, but the present main entrance has been on Elm Street for many years.

58

High Tide Inn is captured here in its natural surroundings. Before this time, it was an Episcopal camp for girls who visited from Bangor and other places to spend a week or two.

A view of the Maine State Fish Hatchery, on Molyneaux Road, c. 1918. Approximately 500 trout and 375,000 salmon were raised that year. It was estimated, in later years, that 37,000 people visited the hatchery during a six-month period. The hatchery closed c. 1942. Today, the property is privately owned and serves as a home.

Firemen gather in front of the old Camden Fire Station on Washington Street. The horse-drawn "Molyneaux" pumper pictured here is now a museum piece at the present Allen F. Payson Fire Station. Camden purchased the pumper immediately after the "great fire," because they needed more up-to-date equipment.

The Camden Public Library (seen here in an early photograph) was designed by Parker Morse Hooper and Charles Loring. The cornerstone was placed on August 17, 1927, and the doors were finally opened to the public on June 11, 1928. It is such a busy place that the building is presently being expanded, with John B. Scholz as the architect.

The back entrance to the Camden Public Library is seen here soon after the library was built. Mary Curtis Bok (later Zimbalist) donated the land and also the statue (called *Two Little Fauns*) seen in the picture.

Camden people used the gymnasium in the Rockport Opera House, treating Rockport as their YMCA. The Rockport gymnasium became too crowded, so Camden decided to build their own gymnasium on Chestnut Street in 1915–16. The building has changed in both appearance and use since this picture was taken.

In 1848, Efraim Harkness sold some of his land to Goose River (now Rockport), for the residents to build the Hoboken Schoolhouse. It served as a school for over one hundred years and is now a floral shop named Hoboken Gardens.

Six
Mountains, Lakes, and Their Views

Viewed here from the ledges is the luxurious private yacht *Lyndonia*, owned by Cyrus H.K. Curtis. It is docked alongside the Camden Yacht Club. The yacht pictured here was the second *Lyndonia*, built for Mr. Curtis because he gave the first one to the government during World War I. The second *Lyndonia* was 230 feet length overall and a sight to behold.

A photograph of Mt. Megunticook, taken by one of Camden/Rockport's best photographers, Will Hall. His studio was on Chestnut Street in Camden, and the author had the pleasure of meeting him before Mr. Hall died in 1935.

A scenic shot of Mt. Battie, taken *c.* 1910 from some undeveloped land on High Street. In this picture, the hotel is visible on the summit, but many more trees have grown on the mountain since then. Mt. Battie was used by the Ku Klux Klan to burn crosses in 1923 and in the early 1930s.

Sherman's Point served as a picnic area when this picture showing the two mountains was taken in 1908. Many houses can already be seen here, nestled beneath Mt. Battie and Mt. Megunticook, but an even greater number of homes have been built since.

A view of the shipyard and both mountains, from the beach on Bayview Street. This photograph was taken *c*. 1918. The popular custom of sending and saving postcards in the early 1900s has meant that many such photographs have been preserved for posterity.

A view of the mountains meeting the sea, photographed in 1922, showing piers on both the east and west side of Camden Harbor.

What a view of the islands in Penobscot Bay and beyond, seen here from the summit of Mt. Battie! The Memorial Tower is to the left, with Sherman's Point to the right.

A close-up view of the tower on the summit of Mt. Battie, showing where the hotel was once situated. It was designed by Parker Morse Hooper and erected in memory of those local people who served in World War I. The Memorial Tower was dedicated on August 20, 1921, in a moving ceremony. The inscription reads: "In grateful recognition of the service of men and women of Camden in the World War, 1914–1918."

An extremely clear view of Camden (and part of Rockport) from Mt. Battie. At the time this photograph was taken there were plenty of house lots and the whole of Eaton's Field in which to build, but today the area is nearly full with lovely homes.

Another view from Mt. Battie, c. 1909, looking toward Sherman's Point. Many raging fires took place on the mountains over the years, but plenty of manpower always turned out and the fires were controlled.

A shot of the Memorial Tower, showing that it was also used for an observation tower. There is a winding set of stone steps leading to the top, where one can get a wonderful view of Camden and Penobscot Bay on a clear day.

This picture shows one of the earlier crosses on Maiden's Cliff. Mt. Megunticook is seen from the swimming area of Megunticook Lake, known today as Barrett's Cove.

The scene is again Mt. Megunticook, seen here from Megunticook Lake in 1920, a few years earlier than the previous photograph.

A romantic photographer captured the moonlight falling on Megunticook Lake in August 1913. In earlier days, it was called Negunticook Lake, and later Canaan Lake.

Held by guy wires, this cross on Maiden's Cliff marks the spot where eleven-year-old Elenora French fell to her death on May 6, 1862. Several crosses have been erected in her memory over the years. Some crosses were destroyed by wind and weather, but some fell victim to vandalism.

The mountains and lakes are beautiful, even in the winter. Of course, with snow and ice on them, they do not see the amount of activity that takes place in the summer.

A view of Megunticook Lake, captured years ago, showing Mt. Megunticook and the islands that dot the lake.

Much of Camden's charm has been attributed to Megunticook Lake, its irregular, wooded shores, and the picturesque islands. The outline of the mountain is seen here reflected on the surface of the lake. The mountain encircles the lake and enhances its beauty. The boats are pictured at the float, ready for some fishing.

An old photograph of Megunticook Lake, with its rocky shore and abundance of trees.

The lower end of Lake Megunticook, pictured with boats tied at the shore and cottages to the left. It was such a calm day that clear reflections of the trees can be seen.

Fernald's Neck stretches out into Lake Megunticook. Balance Rock is located here, where it was left by the glaciers during the Ice Age. There are many trails on the point of land, which is owned by the Nature Conservancy.

This picture was taken in 1919, on a day when the water was a little rough. The view is from the east shore of Megunticook Lake, looking towards some of the islands.

Here we see a canoe beached at Carl Point. It was a great fishing place and not many outboards were used when this picture was taken. Canoes glided serenely over the water and fish were not frightened.

For many years, Mirror Lake has been the source of drinking water for Camden, Rockport, and the surrounding area. It is a beautiful mountain lake, fed by springs and located 350 feet above sea level. This picture was taken in 1931 and shows a couple of rowboats on the lake, but today no activity is allowed on Mirror Lake.

The twin dams of Megunticook Lake—situated at the point where the lake meets the Megunticook River—belonged to William Molyneaux, who bought land there in 1786. He built his home on a point of land and owned both a grist and sawmill. It was once known as Molyneaux Pond. The dams were later used for the Maine State Fish Hatchery when it was located on the site.

The Megunticook River winds peacefully for 3 miles, from the end of the lake to the falls in Camden Harbor. There have been as many as ten dams on the river, each used to power the mills. In the foreground of this picture, taken in 1905, can be seen the Seabright Woven Felt Company, located on the next dam below Molyneaux, called the "Batchelder Privilege." The last mill to go out of business on the river was the Knox Woolen Company, which closed in 1988. A very attractive complex has been built on its site, housing the MBNA New England.

Viewed here from the Camden Public Landing, or Harbor Park, in the late 1800s, the falls cascade over the ledges to Camden Harbor. The hill seen in the background is today the lawn of the Camden Public Library, and the houses pictured here no longer exist.

Hosmer's Pond was first known as Goose Pond, and Goose River, in Rockport, flows from the pond. A group of volunteers got together in 1936, in spite of the Depression, and built a winter recreational spot called the Camden Snow Bowl at Hosmer's Pond.

Seven
Business Districts

Pictured here in 1900 are two ladies walking down Central Street in Rockport, headed toward the village. The business district began here and progressed around the corner. These ladies would have been able to see a view of Goose River as they turned around the corner and crossed the bridge.

This photograph was taken in 1890, after a beautiful ice storm in Camden. All the buildings on the right side of Elm Street burned in the "great fire." The building on the left, which reads "Hunt—caskets and trunks," was moved to upper Elm Street when the Village Green was created in 1928. Chestnut Street ran between those two buildings.

This is a view of Main Street in Camden in 1861, before the "great fire." The first Episcopal Church (center) is today the Camden Farmer's Union. The wooden buildings were all replaced by brick in 1893–94. Wooden sidewalks, dirt roads, and oxen were a common sight in those days.

The morning after the "great fire," which took place on November 10, 1892, Camden's business district lies in charred ruins. Hunt's Shop and the Bay View House can be seen untouched to the left. Businessmen looked it over and made a decision to rebuild immediately.

The rebuilt Main Street was decorated with bunting on Conway Day, August 30, 1906. A boulder was moved from Ogier Hill to the front of the Elm Street School honoring Civil War veteran William Conway.

A view of Main Street, Camden, in 1916, with horses and buggies competing with a few automobiles as modes of transportation. The Civil War Monument can be seen at the top of the hill in Monument Square.

A picture taken from Chestnut Street, in 1911, looking toward the beginning of the Elm Street business district. Chestnut Street was still a dirt road then, and the buildings seen here have long since given way to the Village Green.

Main Street, Camden, before the era of the automobile. Next to the Travelers Inn can be seen a fish market and a store, Collins & Ogier, both of which are located where the Village Restaurant stands today.

84

This view from Monument Square shows all the new brick blocks soon after they were built. The new blocks began where French and Brawn is now located, and all the stores had striped awnings. Automobiles were already common by the time this picture was taken. Perhaps parking problems began then. They have certainly increased over the years.

Cars were already a fixture in Camden when this photograph was taken, but the trolleys were still running. The trees on Harbor Hill look particularly beautiful in this picture.

When this photograph was taken, Main Street, Camden, had it all—bicycles, pedestrians, horse-drawn buggies, and early automobiles. Boynton's Drug Store has not changed in over one hundred years, but the Masonic Block is now the Lord Camden Inn (with its red, white, and blue awnings).

This photograph, taken in 1914, shows the area in the vicinity of the Opera House. People were able to cross the street without the aid of crosswalks, and the "electrics" still went right through the middle of town.

A view of several businesses that once flourished along Main Street, Camden. They include: A.B. Coose (a watch maker), Mrs. A.I. Worthing (ladies' hats, etc.), and S.B. Haskell (clothier). The doorstep shown here on the left was recently uncovered when William Dickey started his custom embroidery shop and restored the building facade.

This *c.* 1940s picture was taken at the junction of Chestnut, Elm, and Main Streets. The "silent policeman" is visible in the middle of Chestnut Street. Crockett's 5 & 10 Cents Store, owned by David Crockett Sr., was a landmark in Camden for many years. It was a favorite store for children and adults alike. His sons, Fred and Dave, took over the store and played an active part in the community.

Shown here is a large section of the business district in Rockport. From left to right are: the Philbrook Building, the Piper Building (once the Swan Inn), and the Carver House. Many businesses have been situated in these buildings over the years.

Eight

Industries

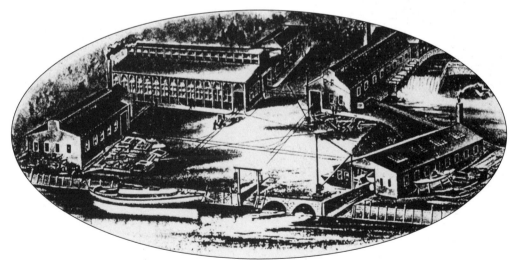

Down on the waterfront was the Camden Anchor Works, started in 1866 by William G. and Horatio E. Alden. Anchors of all sizes, up to 4 tons, were forged there and it was the largest plant of its kind in this country. It was sold in 1901 and combined with a machine shop.

Lime was a prominent industry in Rockport. One of the lime quarries is shown here in 1910, complete with workers and the equipment used to mine the lime rock from the quarry.

Another lime rock quarry in Rockport was the Burgess Quarry, pictured here in 1910. Lime rock was quarried, transported to lime kilns, and burned in order to produce lime.

The shipyard has been a prominent fixture on the east side of the harbor since 1856, and continues to play an important role today.

BURNT LIME

BRINGS QUICKER RESULTS
AND INCREASE IN CROP YIELDS

HAS STOOD THE TEST FOR MORE THAN
TWENTY YEARS

(Is Shipped in 100-lb Cloth Bags)

BUY DIRECT

Get together with your neighbors and your farm bureau. Make up a carload order thus securing the very lowest wholesale price,

$6.50 per Ton

f. o. b. Rockland

and receiving benefit of lowest freight rates

Car shortage and poor transportation service are sure to interfere with deliveries all spring.

ORDER NOW

In case you cannot make up a carload order and your local dealer is unable to supply you with small lots, write our nearest office. We are glad at all times to supply freight rates to your station and further desired information promptly upon application.

Rockland & Rockport Lime Corp.

ROCKLAND, MAINE

**BOSTON
45 Milk Street**

Early advertisement were not that much different from the ones of today.

Lime, being highly inflammable—especially when it came into contact with water—caused many fires. Pictured here is a fire which took place in the lime kilns on the waterfront in Rockport, in 1899.

The Seabright Woven Felt Company was one of several mills located on Megunticook River. In comparison to most rivers, the Megunticook River would be considered a stream, but it only took a small amount of water to turn the water wheels. In 1930, Seabright became the first mill to have automatic looms and also the first peacetime industry to produce items for World War II.

DR. D. P. ORDWAY'S

IMPROVED PLASTER

FAC-SIMILE *D. P. Ordway.*

ESTABLISHED 1881

Widely Extended Use as Remedy for All Rheumatic Ailments, Chronic or Acute

They are a home remedy, applied by the sufferer himself, who knows where the pain is located.

Send for our "MESSAGE OF HOPE." It is a SELF EDUCATOR

PLASTER - 25 Cents Each

THE DR. D. P. ORDWAY PLASTER COMPANY,
CAMDEN, MAINE

Ordway Plaster was packaged with the information shown in this picture. The company sold plaster to customers all over this country and in foreign countries too. Because of the high volume of Ordway's mail, the Camden Post Office became first class.

The workers at the Ordway Plaster factory pose in front of the factory building for this photograph. The building was located in Tannery Lane, on the site of the new Camden Riverhouse Hotel.

Pictured here is the first building of the Knox Woolen Company (now the home of MBNA New England). The industry was incorporated in 1868 and provided employment for many area residents until it closed in 1988. It had the largest payroll in Camden, and actually paid each employee in cash; on pay day, company representatives would go to the bank with a large bag, then return to the mill and separate the money into separate pay envelopes for each employee. The company manufactured the first paper makers' endless belt in this country.

The Knox Mill whistle has been preserved in the Knox Mill Museum in MBNA. It became a time clock for everyone in Camden: it sounded early each morning to summon people to work, it blew to begin and end lunch time, and sounded once more to announce the end of the work day.

The Knox Woolen Company looked like this in 1930, but has had additions over the years. During renovation in 1992, the office building (center) was separated from the main building and moved above the complex on Mechanic Street. It became the home of the *Camden Herald* until it was sold recently to MBNA.

The building of sailing vessels was a major industry in both Camden and Rockport for many years. The four-masted schooner *Charlotte A. Maxwell* is pictured here under construction in the Robert L. Bean Yard in Camden. It was later launched on April 19, 1917.

By the time this picture was taken, the *Charlotte A. Maxwell* had been framed. Measuring an impressive 160 feet in length, she was still smaller than many other schooners of the same period.

Here, the *Charlotte A. Maxwell* is seen after she has been planked. The bow of another boat, being constructed alongside her, is visible in the photograph.

This photograph was taken after the *Charlotte A. Maxwell* had been completed and just before she was to slide down the ways. The Eastern Steamship Wharf is just beyond the edge of the picture to the left.

Another four-masted schooner, the *Helen Barnet Gring*, is pictured here being launched on July 29, 1919, near the end of the sailing vessel era.

This picture shows Camden's business district, with the Camden Anchor Works featured prominently by the waterfront. Few boats were in the inner harbor on this particular day.

The launch of the *Frederick Billings* took place in Rockport on August 11, 1885. Constructed by Carleton, Norwood, & Company, the vessel made headlines as she was the second-largest ever to be built on this continent. She was 281 feet long and her anchor weighed 6,000 pounds.

The Knowlton Brothers' Foundry is pictured here in 1907. The company had the capability to manufacture just about anything a vessel could need—capstans, windlasses, pumps, winches, steering wheels, blocks, etc. Fires frequently consumed foundry buildings such as these and the only one remaining today is the Knowlton Brothers building, constructed in 1911 and recently remodeled by MBNA New England.

Lobstering has been an active business in Camden and Rockport for many decades. This picture shows lobster traps hauled for the winter.

Joseph Brewster began his business with a team of horses and a wagon. A wonderful, hard-working man with a pleasing personality, he created a very successful business.

As Mr. Brewster's business continued to grow, he built a new shirt factory in 1912. The jubilant workers pictured outside the factory in 1919 are celebrating the end of World War I and welcoming "the boys" home with a parade.

Nine
Churches

The steeple of the first Episcopal Church rises behind the Civil War Monument. Today, the Camden Farmers Union has its business in that building. The steps of the second Methodist Church can be seen to the left.

A photograph of the interior of the First Congregational Church in Camden, *c.* 1910. William E. Carleton, artist/decorator, stamped the back of the picture, so we can probably assume that the fancy work had been done by him. The simplicity of the interior is noticeable today and is similar to the design of the Congregational churches built by the Puritans in the seventeenth century.

This is a view of the exterior of the First Congregational Church, first built in 1834. The front had two entrances and the steeple was on the roof, instead of on the side of the edifice as it is today.

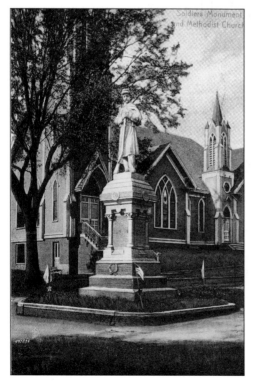

The Methodists of Camden built and dedicated the church shown here on December 19, 1894, after the "great fire" consumed their first church on Washington Street. The cost of the new building was $15,000. Today, a new church has been built on John Street, for both Camden and Rockport parishioners, and the building shown in this picture is a condominium.

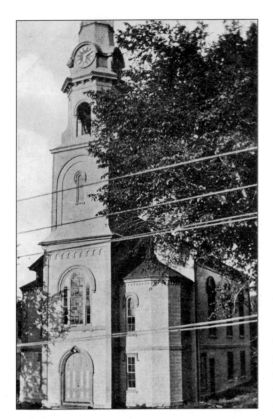

The Chestnut Street Baptist Church, which first opened its doors in 1837. The exterior was later remodeled. Formerly painted yellow, the church was repainted white *c.* 1928.

The St. Thomas Episcopal Church on Chestnut Street held its first service in this typical English-style building on February 14, 1924. Also seen here is the manse. The first church, which was situated on Mountain Street, was sold.

The "spite church," or Union Hall, was located on Paul's Hill in Rockport. Today Paul's Hill is known either as Route 1, Commercial Street, or Richards' Hill. A traditional local story has been passed down telling how Benjamin Paul went to church with his family and dog. When the minister insisted that the dog leave the church, Mr. Paul left with his family and dog. Shortly afterwards, *c.* 1890, Paul built Union Hall, where anyone was welcome . . . including his dog.

The Vesper Hill Chapel is located in Rockport, in a beautiful outdoor setting where the ocean is visible from the chapel. Helene Bok designed and commissioned the building of the "children's chapel." She carefully planned the gardens, which were planted with a variety of Biblical flowers. It is used and enjoyed by many to this day.

Our Lady of Good Hope Catholic Church was built on Union Street in Camden in 1909. Previously, the nearest Catholic church had been 8 miles away in Rockland. Many summer residents employed Irish women, and donated money to build a Catholic church so that their employees could attend mass in Camden.

Ten

Recreation

The card reads: "You should spend your vacation in Camden, Maine." Thousands of people do just that every year, not only in the summer but during the other seasons too. On a recent television show, it was declared that Camden was one of the best three places in the United States to live or vacation.

Cyrus H.K. Curtis purchased a prime spot on Camden Harbor and built the Camden Yacht Club in 1912. He presented the club to the inhabitants of Camden in 1926, to be used as a community house. It was designed by one of Maine's most noted architects, John Calvin Stevens.

This photograph was taken in 1897, and shows a group having a good time at Lake City. A large hotel, the Lake City Inn, was built at Megunticook Lake in 1893 but was destroyed in a conflagration only three years later.

Balance Rock, situated on a piece of land called Fernald's Neck, was left there by a glacier during the Ice Age. Every boy who has been to see it over the years has tried to toppled it over. Balance Rock does not move and it remains a great attraction in the picnic area.

The Megunticook Golf Club is located in Rockport. It has been a popular place for golfing, tennis, and socializing for many years.

The CCC camps were shelters built during the Depression for people to enjoy outings in the Sagamore Picnic Area. It now is part of the Camden Hills State Park, located on the opposite side of the camping area to the summit of Mt. Battie.

In both Camden and Rockport, there are many places to sit on the rocks and enjoy a picturesque view of mountains and water. What peaceful, serene places to have lunch or read a book!

For many years, there have been "day-trippers" in Camden. People can buy a ticket for an hour-long or all-day ride in a boat to view Camden, Rockport, and other places along Penobscot Bay.

Weekly races were held by the Camden Yacht Club involving a class of sailboats called HAJs . The boats were privately owned by young adults and originally purchased in Finland, by Alvah Anderson, in the 1930s.

This is a view of Sherman's Point—once a beautiful spot on the bay for family gatherings and picnics. The area was sold by the Town of Camden and many fine homes have since been built there.

Captain Frank Swift began a windjammer fleet in 1936 and continued these cruising vacations for the public until 1961. The *Mercantile* was built in Maine in 1916, and its LOA (length overall) was 80 feet. Some of the vessels in the windjammer fleet were built as early as the 1880s. They still operate from Camden Harbor for vacation cruises.

In 1936, volunteers constructed the Camden Snow Bowl at Hosmer's Pond, for winter recreation. The house pictured here made the skaters more comfortable while they put on and took off their skates. It was affectionately called "Hotel Rockport."

Each year for six years, a queen and her ladies-in-waiting reigned over the Snow Bowl Carnival. In 1938, Mary Bryant was queen and her ladies were Nancy Hobbs, Elizabeth Pitcher, Lea Fransen, and Winona Robinson. They are pictured here on the stage of the Camden Opera House, where the Coronation Ball took place.

Skiing has always been very popular on Ragged Mountain, during the Snow Bowl, with people getting to the summit via the ski tow. This photograph was taken near the summit.

Several movies have been filmed in Camden and Rockport. *Peyton Place* was one of the most memorable ones, filmed in 1957 with Lana Turner in the leading role. Hundreds of people from this area signed on as extras and many are pictured in this scene in front of the Knox Woolen Company (the name of the company was changed for the movie).

Ice boating used to be a popular (and very cold) sport in Camden and Rockport. This photograph was taken in 1936, on the Lily Pond in Rockport, and the author rode many times on the boat pictured, as it was built by her father for his family.

Chestnut Street, Camden, was closed off for sledding in the winter, from Limerock to Frye Street. In 1937 Milton Dyer had a bobsled and he and the author would start from their home on Chestnut Street (near Cedar Street) and sled all the way down the street, past Camden National Bank and part of the way up Bayview Street. There were no brakes but they never had an accident— maybe they were just lucky.

Just to sit on a park bench on a nice day and look at beautiful Rockport Harbor was and is perfect recreation for many people.

Fishing has always been popular recreation for many. Camden has been blessed with many beautiful lakes and ponds. You never know when you will feel a bite on the line, and whether it will be a salmon, bass, pickerel, perch, trout, or just a tree limb that your hook has snagged.

Eleven
Parades

World War I soldiers are pictured here marching in a huge parade, following their arrival back home after the war. It was called "Welcome The Boys Home Parade" and was held in August 1919.

The whole of Camden's business district was decorated in red, white, and blue bunting for the parade, which marked the end of World War I. It must have looked both very festive and patriotic.

Automobiles were decorated to serve as floats in the same parade. A crowd gathers here in front of the Camden Post Office as the parade proceeds up Chestnut Street.

The Red Cross was represented by the decorated automobile shown here. The Red Cross served the armed forces well in both World Wars I and II.

A horse-drawn wagon acts as a float in the parade. It features a spinning wheel, wool, and a sheep, and the decoration is quite fancy.

The crew from the Robert Bean Yard march in the parade, all with caps and flags and some with their working tools. Behind them is a mock-up of a vessel being built, paraded here as a float.

This photograph shows servicemen at the same parade marching up Main Street, headed toward Mountain Street. The whole town of Camden turned out to see it. Camden's population was then about 3,400.

Following behind the parade are horses and buggies. During public occasions everyone dressed in their finest in those days, even if they were just watching a parade.

Another gigantic parade formed on August 30, 1906, to honor William Conway, a Civil War hero. He was ordered to lower the flag at the Pensacola Naval Yard so that the Confederates could take over, but he refused. Forty-one years after his death, Conway was honored by Camden with a boulder and parade. When the boulder reached the bottom of Chestnut Street, it had to be turned and hauled up Elm Street.

The Conway boulder finally arrived at its destination in front of the Elm Street School. One can hardly believe it weighed 30 tons. Parades were once major events in Camden.

Twelve
Parks

The Library Amphitheatre, previously known as the Garden Theatre, is pictured here in 1934, seen from Atlantic Avenue near the gate houses. The outdoor amphitheatre has been used for plays, weddings, band concerts, and high school graduations. It was designed by the noted Boston architect Fletcher Steele.

Oakland Park was built in 1902 and maintained by the Rockland, Thomaston, and Camden Street Railway. The fare on the trolley cars earned the company enough profit to build and maintain a wonderful park, free to all and popular with families.

The entrance to Oakland Park was quite elegant. The trolley went from Camden and Rockport down to the park entrance, taking many families to enjoy a day out.

Everyone loved a band concert. As you can see, young and old alike attended the concert shown in this picture. A variety of other activities, including ball games, took place in Oakland Park.

The pond at Oakland Park was certainly an attraction. Walkways by the pond provided a way to absorb all the beauty.

Rockland, Me. Entrance Oakland Park.

Another view of the entrance to the park. Oakland Park was enjoyed by thousands for nearly forty years. After World War II, it was purchased by a private owner, and a public dance hall and rollerskating rink provided entertainment. Tourist cabins are located there today.

The ladies shown here are in their finest dresses and hats. Whether out for a picnic, a ball game, or a concert, everyone in those days dressed to look nice but not necessarily for comfort.